WEATHER LEGENDS

WEATHER LEGENDS

NATIVE AMERICAN LORE AND THE SCIENCE OF WEATHER

Carole Garbuny Vogel

The Millbrook Press
Brookfield, Connecticut

Cover photograph © Visuals Unlimited, Inc.
Photographs courtesy of © Larry Mayer: p. 12; Visuals Unlimited, Inc.: pp. 21 (© Mundy Hackett), 26 (© Mark
E. Gibson), 64 (© Science/VU); National Park Service: p. 31 (© Richard Frear); Photo Researchers, Inc.: pp. 38
(© Rod Planck), 45 (© 1991 Kent Wood), 52 (© 1995 S. R. Maglione), 57 (© Yva Momatiuk & John Eastcott), 63
(© Nuridsany et Perennou), 70 (© Howard Bluestein), 72 (© Tom McHugh, 1978)

Library of Congress Cataloging-in-Publication Data
Vogel, Carole Garbuny.
Weather legends: Native American lore and the science of weather / Carole Garbuny Vogel.
p. cm.
Includes bibliographical references and index.
ISBN 0-7613-1900-X (lib. bdg.)
1. Indians of North America—Folklore. 2. Weather—Folklore. 3. Weather—Juvenile literature. [1. Indians of
North America—Folklore. 2. Weather—Folklore. 3. Folklore—North America. 4. Weather.] I. Title: Native
American lore and the science of weather. II. Title.
E98.F6   V66   20001
398.2'089'97—dc21   00-051973

Published by The Millbrook Press, Inc.
2 Old New Milford Road
Brookfield, Connecticut 06804
www.millbrookpress.com

To the memory of my father, Dr. Max Garbuny,
who inspired my love of natural phenomena and passed on to me his writing talent.

ACKNOWLEDGMENTS

I wish to thank Maja Groff, a student at Harvard University and native of rainy North Vancouver Island, for her capable assistance with the myth research. I would also like to thank my sister, Ellen Garbuny, for her help in tracking down obscure legends.

I was delighted to work for a third time with my editor, Laura Walsh, whose keen insight is gratefully acknowledged. Thanks also to my agent, Tracey Adams of McIntosh and Otis, who consistently manages to make the business of writing fun.

As always I am completely indebted to my writer friends, Florence Harris and Joyce A. Nettleton, for their excellent critiques. I truly don't know what I would do without the support and wisdom of my husband, Mark A. Vogel, who double-checks and triple-checks my science facts and takes care of dinner when I am too swamped with work.

Finally, I am most appreciative of the Native American storytellers who created, nurtured, and passed on the beautiful legends that I have adapted in this book.

INTRODUCTION

My earliest memory is of an unusually violent thunderstorm that occurred before I turned three years old. My older sister, Vivian, and I watched the lightning display from our parents' bedroom window. We lived on the third floor of an apartment building in Pittsburgh, Pennsylvania. I remember being awestruck by the brilliant streaks of light that slashed the city sky. Equally impressive was the almost constant crash of thunder, but I recall being unafraid.

My father was a physicist, and he soothed my sister and me with scientific explanations. He spoke about positive ions and negative ions and about how opposites attract. I barely understood a word he uttered, but I remember thinking that someday I would understand. Each time lightning flashed, Dad would begin to count until we heard the rumble of thunder. Then he did a quick computation aloud and announced how far away the lightning had struck. Dad lived to be eighty-six years old, and his fascination with severe weather never faded.

Weather plays a major role in the lives of everyone on Earth today. It impacts the clothes we wear, the food we eat, the homes we live in, and our outdoor activities. And so it was for the Native Americans who lived in North America long before European settlement.

Modern science provides us with complex explanations for meteorological events and the tools for forecasting weather. From simple equipment such as weather vanes and rain gauges, to satellites that track hurricanes from space, and Doppler radar that provides early warning of tornadoes and flash floods, humanity has never been better equipped to prepare for severe weather. We simply turn on the television or radio or check the Internet for the latest weather update.

In ancient times, these tools didn't exist. Native Americans viewed the events taking place in the sky as a blend of physical and spiritual parts. The sun, wind, and clouds were believed to be living entities with a spirit and personality of their own. Humans and animals interacted with these and other spirit beings who inhabited the Earth and sky. The actions of individual humans or entire tribes sometimes had dire consequences on the weather. Punishment for provoking spirits often came in the form of floods, severe storms, or prolonged drought.

Weather Legends retells the native legends of murderous serpents, immense sky warriors, and kindly spirit beings, and how these entities are linked to the amazing weather dramas that take place around us. The book also gives a brief summary of how scientists understand the meteorological forces that dominate the atmosphere and create the weather we experience.

I hope that understanding both the scientific and sacred accounts of weather will contribute to your enjoyment and knowledge of the events taking place in the sky above.

Carole G. Vogel
Lexington, Massachusetts

CONTENTS

FLOOD

CHIPPEWA-OJIBWA

MINNESOTA, WISCONSIN, AND
THE PROVINCE OF ONTARIO

In the beginning, when spirit beings still lived among people, Manabozho was the protector of the human race. He was the son of an earthly woman and the Great Spirit, Manitou. Manabozho taught the people how to hunt and catch fish, how to plant crops, and how to make sugar from the sap of the maple tree. He shared with them the secret of fire so they could prepare hot meals and warm themselves on cold nights.

Manabozho lived in a lodge with his young cousin, whom he treated as a son. One day Manabozho returned home from a long journey to find his beloved cousin missing. He called out the little boy's name but received no answer. So Manabozho went outside to look for the boy. There he discovered the trail of his enemy, the Great Serpent, and realized that the giant snake had kidnapped the boy.

Manabozho grabbed his bow and arrow and followed the trail. It led him across several high mountains and steep valleys, over a fast-moving river, and through a dark forest. At last it brought him to the edge of a deep, gloomy lake.

At the bottom of the lake dwelled the Great Serpent with his many companions and servants. All were terrible monsters with evil sprits and snakelike forms. They obeyed the Great Serpent without hesitation.

Manabozho peered into the water, and in the middle of all the vile creatures he spied the Great Serpent. The serpent's immense head was blood-red in color with fierce eyes of blazing fire. Hard, glistening scales of every shade covered his body. To Manabozho's horror he saw that the serpent's massive form was coiled around the lifeless body of the precious young boy.

In sadness and anger, Manabozho vowed revenge. He decided to make the lake so hot that the Great Serpent and his ruthless companions could not remain. They would be forced to find shelter in the cool shade of the trees growing on the lake bank. There Manabozho would dispense his own justice.

Manabozho asked the clouds to vanish from the sky, the winds to cease their cooling breeze, and the sun to shine unremittingly on the lake. Manabozho then picked up his bow and arrow and found the coolest, shadiest patch of forest, knowing that this was where the Great Serpent would come. Manabozho then transformed himself into a broken stump so the evil spirits would not detect his presence.

Soon the winds stopped blowing, the clouds disappeared, and the sun beat down relentlessly on the lake. The water became warm, and then hot. When it began to steam and hiss, the vile creatures poked their heads above the surface and scanned the shore. Sensing a trap, they searched for signs of Manabozho and listened for his footsteps. But they found no trace of him.

"Manabozho must be asleep," they decided, and plunged back into the scalding water.

Before long the lake began to bubble and boil. Immense waves of blistering hot water crashed against the rocks along the shore.

The heat became too much for the Great Serpent to tolerate. Slowly he emerged from the lake's depths. His blood-red head shimmered a deep crimson, and the fire in his eyes burned white-hot. Had he been capable of spitting fire, flames surely would have leapt from his mouth. As he slithered onto the banks of the lake, his cronies trailed after him, filling the shore with their foul-smelling hulks.

When the creatures spied the broken trunk, they immediately suspected that it was Manabozho. So one of them wrapped its body around the stump and tried to uproot it. But Manabozho held on fast. After a few minutes the creatures gave up and slunk away to find shady places to rest.

The Great Serpent slipped into the forest and looped his gargantuan body around several majestic trees. Soon he and his companions fell fast asleep, leaving one particularly savage fiend on the lookout for Manabozho.

When the guard was looking the other way, Manabozho silently picked up his bow and arrow and carefully took aim. Then he shot the Great Serpent in the heart. The serpent awoke with an ear-splitting shriek. His face contorted in pain, the Great Serpent dragged his wounded body back into the lake, where his worried companions joined him.

When the serpent realized that he had been mortally wounded, he and his cohorts vented their rage on Manabozho. They forced the lake to expand and rise from its depth. In giant waves, the water cascaded over the banks and poured onto the forest floor.

Writhing in agony, the Great Serpent rode the crest of the first mighty wave. The color had drained from his head and scales, but his eyes still burned like fiery coals. Alongside the serpent raced his loyal followers, hissing loudly, vowing vengeance.

Retreating from the onslaught, Manabozho thought of the men, women, and children who lived in the countryside. He also thought of the spirit beings, like Beaver, Otter, and Muskrat, who lived among the humans. Quickly Manabozho raced to their villages and warned everyone to flee to the mountains. As the people and spirit beings fled, water filled the valleys and swallowed the highest hills. Now it clawed at the sides of the mountains, and Manabozho urged everyone to climb higher.

The water rose higher still. Soon it gobbled up every mountain except for the highest one, where Manabozho stood surrounded by desperate people and spirit beings. Manabozho hastily gathered up trees and lashed them together to form an enormous raft. Just as the floodwaters licked the mountaintop, Manabozho guided the last of the people and spirit beings onto the raft.

For a week, Manabozho and his charges floated alone on the water. The people begged him to disperse the water and renew the Earth. But to repair the world, Manabozho first needed a few grains of earth from beneath the floodwaters.

Beaver volunteered to dive to the bottom of the floodwaters and retrieve some earth. Although she was warned of the danger, she dove into the deluge. As the minutes and then hours passed with no sign of Beaver, the anxious people realized that she could not have survived her mission. Her body eventually floated to the surface, and the people opened her paws. There was no earth inside them.

Next Otter offered to try. He plunged into the murky waters and was gone longer than Beaver. At first when his body resurfaced, the people thought he had survived. But like Beaver, Otter had perished, and there was no earth in his paws.

The people were becoming desperate. Who could save them? Finally Muskrat stepped forward. He took a deep breath before diving into the water and disappeared for an even longer period than Otter. The people thought he would never return.

Suddenly, someone spotted a speck in the water. Slowly it moved closer to the raft. It was Muskrat, so tired he could barely swim. The people pulled him aboard, where he gave one final gasp and died from exhaustion. Inside his paw Muskrat grasped a few clumps of earth.

Manabozho took the precious grains and laid them out in the sun. When they were dry, he pulverized them into tiny bits of dust and blew the dust over the water.

Instantly the floodwaters began to subside, and soon the mountains appeared and then the hills and the valleys. The newly emerged land showed no trace of the flood except for a thick layer of mud, which was the dust that Manabozho had blown over the water.

And the evil spirits? Although their master, the Great Serpent, had died from his wound, his followers returned to the bottom of the lake. They were so frightened of Manabozho they never dared to leave their home again.

Since the time of Noah, floods have plagued humankind. Sometimes torrential rains or rapid snowmelts trigger the flooding. In coastal areas, high winds can whip up wave heights 10 to 15 feet, sending water barreling ashore. Hurricanes create storm surges, swiftly rising tides that can raise the ocean level 15 feet or more. Tsunamis, volcanic eruptions, landslides, and bursting dams can all produce tremendous floods capable of snuffing out thousands of lives in minutes.

Perhaps a flash flood inspired the flood myth described on the preceding pages. Flash floods occur with amazing swiftness and little warning. They frequently develop when thunderstorms stall at the top of a deep valley or canyon, producing drenching rains. The water soaks into the soil and spills into gullies and streams. Like a sponge filled to capacity, the ground becomes waterlogged. Rainwater streaks across the land and tumbles into the already swollen waterways. The gullies and streams become frenzied currents that overwhelm their banks and careen into the river draining the valley. The river turns into a quickly rising torrent. Rampaging downstream, it jumps its banks and demolishes everything in its path.

One of the most deadly flash floods in American history occurred in Rapid City, South Dakota, on the night of June 9, 1972. A string of thunderstorms hunkered down over the eastern slopes of the Black Hills, more than 20 miles upstream from Rapid City. Nearly 15 inches of rain poured from the sky in less than six hours. The water spilled into Rapid Creek, changing the 15-foot-wide bubbling trout brook into a raging river. The floodwaters roared down the slopes, straight toward Canyon Lake Dam, near the outskirts of the city.

The mayor issued a warning, broadcast on local radio stations, for residents to abandon areas vulnerable to flooding. But many residents ignored the warning. Having experienced high water before, they believed that moving furniture, appliances, and other valuables from the basement to a higher level was the only necessary precaution. They did not consider fleeing their homes until it was too late.

Flood debris clogged the dam's spillway, trapping the floodwaters. The water behind the dam rapidly climbed 11 to 12 feet higher than normal. Unable to withstand the pressure, the dam collapsed, creating a giant flood wave. The wall of water thundered toward Rapid City.

The flood struck quickly and ferociously. Horrified witnesses watched as men, women, and children were trapped in their homes by the wild, swirling water and swept away. In all, 238 people died and 3,000 others were injured.

RAINBOW

PAPAGO

SOUTHWEST

Long ago when the Earth was new, two families lived side by side in a little desert village. Together they planted seeds in the field, collected cactus fruit, tended their cattle, and gathered acorns in the mountains. Both families had many children.

In one family there was a little boy whose favorite playmate was a little girl from the other family. As the years flew by, the children grew and the friendship between the boy and the girl ripened into love.

The boy was now a strong and handsome young man. But he was also slow and lazy. He never helped out in the fields or joined in the hunt. The girl was a beautiful young woman who understood the boy. She didn't mind that he shirked his responsibilities. When the boy and girl were together the days seemed bright and smiles came easily. Happiness prevailed.

Before long, the time came for the girl's parents to find her a suitable husband. They found several young men who would be good matches. These were young men who worked their own fields and paraded into the village on wild horses they had captured and tamed.

The young men were known for their willingness to work and their eagerness to compete in games and races. The girl's parents praised their skill, drive, and bravery.

One day the girl's mother asked her which of the young men she would choose for a husband. The girl replied that she would have none but the carefree boy who had been her friend since childhood.

Trouble followed. The mother recited all the boy's flaws, which her daughter knew well. The boy was lazy. He preferred to lie in the shade than toil in the fields. He would rather gaze at the birds than run races or play games. He had no interest in capturing his own horse, much less learning to ride. To make matters worse, his family had little. If the girl married him she would come to depend on her parents. And that would be unfair to her brothers.

So the issue was decided. The girl would marry a young man from a village on the far side of the distant mountains.

The girl stormed outside and found her friend lounging in the shade. She sat down next to him and immediately felt calm again. The boy and girl talked and watched butterflies flit by. They were so happy in each other's company that they almost forgot that the girl would soon leave forever.

It was only when the wedding preparations began that the boy fully realized what the separation would mean. No longer could he and the girl talk or spend time together. He would be terribly lonely without her. Now the days seemed cold and dark. The boy rarely smiled.

The boy shared his sorrow with the girl. She promised never to forget him and to send him messages. But how could they communicate? The villages were far apart, and huge mountains would block smoke signals.

Together the boy and girl tried to find a way. They experimented with shiny rocks that reflected sunlight that could be seen from great distances. But they realized the mountains would block the light, too.

The boy and girl asked the birds if they would carry messages back and forth. Although the birds felt sorry for the two young people, they declined. The mountains were simply too far away for an easy flight.

The preparations for the wedding feast were almost complete when the boy disappeared. He returned a few days later, carrying a basket filled with brightly colored feathers. The feathers came in brilliant colors—red, orange, yellow, green, blue, indigo, and violet. They sparkled so radiantly they looked as though they were on fire.

The boy explained to the girl that he had journeyed far south to visit a medicine woman. The medicine woman had given him the feathers and precise directions for using them. As the boy gave the girl her share of the feathers, he told her what to do.

Not long afterward, the girl married and moved to the far side of the mountains. She brought along the beautiful feathers and guarded them vigilantly.

The first time a big rainstorm came, the girl thought of the boy. She took out the feathers and waited for the rain to stop. As soon as the sun peeked out from behind the clouds, the girl raced outside and held the feathers high over her head with one hand. Slowly she began to dance. When the sunlight hit the feathers the colors flowed up into the sky.

Then, as the girl watched, she saw the same colors streaming toward her from the other side of the mountains. The girl felt happy because she knew the boy was thinking of her.

To this day people feel joy when they see a rainbow. The dazzling colors carry love across the sky. Sometimes the rainbow appears in two parts. This happens when the girl becomes so excited that she dances with the feathers in both hands.

A European superstition claims that any woman who passes under a rainbow will turn into a man. And any man making the same journey will be transformed into a woman. These notions, however, can never be tested. It is impossible to go beneath a rainbow's arch and come through the other side.

A rainbow is a band of brilliant colors, which may curve across the sky after a rain. The two essential ingredients for rainbows are sunlight and water droplets. Rainbows appear when sunlight shines through water droplets lingering in the air.

Although sunlight seems to be colorless, it is actually a mixture of colors. Light travels in waves that are somewhat like the waves in water. Imagine a lake with small waves that are closely spaced. Along comes a wind that whips up the water. The waves become larger and farther apart.

The top of a wave is called its crest, and the distance between two crests is a wavelength. When waves come close together, they have a short wavelength. When they are spaced far apart, they have a long wavelength. You can think of each color of light as a series of waves. Each color has its own specific wavelength. The wavelength of red light is much longer than that of blue light.

As sunlight enters a water drop, the drop acts like a miniature prism. It separates and spreads out the sunlight into a band of different colors by bending the rays of each wavelength a different amount. The inner surface of the drop then reflects the different bands of light, bouncing them back in the direction from which they came. As they exit the drop, the bands of light are bent again, spreading the colors even more.

Although a great variety of colors make up a rainbow, we tend to think of it as being composed of only seven major ones—red, orange, yellow, green, blue, indigo, and violet. Red appears on the outside and violet on the inside. To remember the order of the colors of a rainbow, just think of the name ROY G. BIV. Each letter in the name is the first letter of a color.

In a typical rainstorm, millions of drops may act as prisms and create a beautiful rainbow. Larger drops produce rainbows with brighter and more distinct colors than smaller drops.

Rainbows always appear in the direction opposite the sun. Sometimes a second, less brilliant rainbow spans the outside of the first. The sequence of the color is reversed in the fainter rainbow. This second rainbow forms when sunlight is reflected twice before emerging from the raindrops. From the ground, the most of a rainbow you will ever see is half a circle. The arc of a rainbow is largest at sunrise and sunset when the sun is at the horizon.

Rainbows are rarely seen in winter because water droplets in the sky freeze into tiny ice crystals. Ice crystals scatter light but don't reflect it as water drops do.

SUN

PIMA

SOUTHWEST

Before the world began there was only darkness and water. From time to time the darkness would clump together, then pull apart, and clump together and pull apart. This occurred again and again, until finally it formed a man.

The man existed in the darkness until he became aware of himself. He began to think, and he understood that he was there for a purpose. He placed his hand over his heart and felt something hard. He gave a tug and from his chest came a large stick. He used this stick to guide himself in the dark and to rest upon when he tired.

Soon the man realized that he could craft other things from his body. To keep himself company, he formed little ants and placed them on the stick.

The stick oozed gum, and the ants rolled the gum into a little ball. When the man discovered the ball, he knew he could make something wonderful from it. So he placed it under his foot and began to roll it in the darkness. As he rolled the ball it became bigger and bigger. Eventually it became the world. The man then called himself the maker of the world.

Next, the man pulled a rock from his body and broke the rock into hundreds of small pieces. He scattered the rocks in the sky and turned them into stars to light the darkness. But beautiful as they were, the stars did not shine brightly enough to illuminate the dark.

The man brought forth more rock from his body and turned it into the moon and the Milky Way galaxy. To the man's disappointment, they shone only faintly. Sadly, he realized that there was nothing inside him bright enough to light up the world.

So he leaned on his stick and thought for a long while. Finally he decided to make two large bowls. He filled one with water and used the other to cover it. Then he sat down and stared at the bowl. Concentrating with all his might, he willed the water to turn into light. And as he willed it, his desire was fulfilled. The water in the bowl became the sun. Its beams shone through the cracks where the two bowls came together.

The man removed the sun from the bowls and threw it to the east. The sun stayed exactly where it landed. So the man tried throwing the sun to the north—but again the sun stayed put in the sky. The man also tried the south and west, but to no avail. Finally he slung the sun to the east again. This time it touched the ground and bounced back into the sky. At once it began to travel around the world and has not stopped to this day. Each morning, however, if you look carefully you can see that the sun must bounce off the ground in the east to continue its journey.

About 4.6 billion years ago on the outskirts of the Milky Way galaxy there was a cloud of gas and dust, billions of miles across. The cloud began to collapse in on itself and take the shape of a flat, spinning disk.

Within the disk, bits of the gas and dust drifted into each other. They stuck together and formed minute pebbles. The pebbles bumped together to form bigger clumps, and the bigger clumps collided to produce even larger ones. These large pieces had sufficient gravity to attract additional material. Gravity is the invisible "glue" that holds the universe together.

The hottest and greatest amount of matter swarmed to the center of the disk, where it became the sun. The leftover material in the outer, cooler part of the disk crunched together. Over time it became the planets, moons, and cosmic rubble such as asteroids and comets.

It took roughly 25 million years for the Earth to emerge. When it was complete, the planet was a hot and molten sphere. Its heat came partly from the decay of radioactive elements within the Earth, and partly from leftover heat released during the collisions that formed the planet.

Shortly after the Earth formed, the heavier, denser materials inside it, such as iron, sank to the center. Lighter, less dense materials floated toward the surface. As the Earth started to cool, a hard crust solidified on the surface. Gases trapped beneath the crust escaped through volcanoes and built up an atmosphere, an ocean of air cloaking the planet.

Today the atmosphere stretches more than 600 miles above the surface of the Earth. Nearly four-fifths of the atmosphere is nitrogen, about one-fifth is oxygen, and the rest consists of small amounts of water vapor, carbon dioxide, and other gases. The atmosphere also contains dust, soot, and a wide variety of other tiny particles.

The molecules in the atmosphere move constantly. They spread upward and outward, but gravity keeps the majority from drifting into space. Three-fourths of the atmosphere is squeezed into a layer about 6 to 10 miles thick above the Earth's surface. This lowest layer of the atmosphere, the troposphere, contains the air we breathe, and it is where weather takes place. Weather is what is happening in the air at any one place and time.

You live at the bottom of this vast ocean of air. On clear, sunny days when you peer up, you see blue sky. The blue color is caused by sunlight bouncing off air molecules and dust particles above and around you. In the previous chapter you learned that sunlight looks colorless, but is actually a mixture of the colors. When raindrops or other prisms unscramble sunlight, the colors fan out in a rainbow, a broad band that you can see.

This mixture of light of different wavelengths travels all together for the approximately eight minutes it takes a ray of sunlight to cross the space between the sun and the Earth. But when the sunlight enters the Earth's atmosphere, gas molecules and dust scatter the light. The short wavelength violet and blue colors are scattered most easily. On clear days the sky appears blue because wherever you look in the sky you see blue light that has been scattered away from the sun. The sun itself appears to be yellow. Light with longer wavelengths is not scattered as much and passes mostly unhindered through the atmosphere to the ground.

At sunrise and sunset, the sun appears close to the horizon. To reach you, sunlight must pass through more of the atmosphere than when it is overhead. This additional atmosphere permits only the long wavelength light to reach you at these times. If you look toward the sun you see red, orange, and yellow. If you look away from the sun you see dark skies.

At night, without the sun's rays and away from the lights of civilization, the sky appears black except for the light of the moon, stars, and other objects in space.

WIND

MI'KMAQ (MICMAC)

NORTHERN AND EASTERN MAINE

AND THE ATLANTIC PROVINCES OF CANADA

Long ago an old man and woman resided along the ocean shore with their two grown sons. The older son was married with young children of his own. In that time a married son often lived in the same home as his parents and worked together with his father to feed the family. This family subsisted mainly on fish from the sea. And of all the fish they caught, they liked eels the most.

One day the weather turned stormy. Night and day a fierce wind blew, thrashing up the waves to great heights. Fishing became too dangerous, and soon the family had nothing to eat. Day after day the young children cried from hunger. Finally, the old man told the elder of his sons to walk far beyond their home and search the shore for dead fish that might have been swept up on the beach.

The son ventured off. He made slow progress because the wind blew so hard. After several hours he still had found no fish. Onward he trudged until eventually he reached Rocky

Point, a ledge of immense, sharp boulders jutting out into the ocean. Here the wind blew the most intensely, and enormous waves stretched up from the sea. The young man could barely stand. As he struggled to stay on his feet he spied a solitary form in the distance.

There on the farthest rock stood a large bird, flapping his mighty wings. It was the Storm King, whipping up the wind and seas, and bringing misery to the Mi'kmaq people.

The young man realized that he had a chance to outwit the powerful creature. He called to the big bird and addressed him as "my grandfather," a sign of great respect.

"Are you cold?" asked the young man.

"No," answered the Storm King.

"You are cold," insisted the man. "I can see you shivering. Let me help you ashore."

"All right," agreed the Storm King.

So the man clambered over the slippery ledge to the very last rock where the Storm King stood. Gently he placed the large bird on his back and carefully retraced his steps. When he had almost reached the shore, the man tripped deliberately. But he made it appear as though his fall was an accident. The poor bird toppled onto the rocks and his right wing was fractured.

"I am so sorry," said the man. And he immediately set the bone and bound the injured wing to keep it from moving. "You must keep your wings still until the broken one is healed."

"All right," said the Storm King.

"Stay here and I will come back with food," said the man.

The walk home was much easier. The wind had stopped and the sea had calmed. The man's father and brother had already begun fishing again. Eel fishing was especially good, as the eels were plentiful and easily speared. Soon the family had full bellies. And as promised, the man brought food to the Storm King each day.

But even a good thing can sour. The calm weather lasted for days on end. After a while, scum formed on the surface of the quiet water. The thick, filmy layer prevented the old man and his sons from seeing into the water. They could not find any eels.

So on his next visit to the Storm King, the young man examined the injured wing.

"It is healed enough to permit a gentle motion," he said. "You must flap your wings slowly but steadily."

And the Storm King did. This had the intended outcome. A light breeze rippled the water and carried away the scum. Once more the people fished and fed in peace.

Billions of air molecules are constantly pushing on you and bouncing off your body. At sea level, the atmosphere presses on you with a force of nearly 15 pounds per square inch. It doesn't crush you because your body is adapted to withstand the pressure.

Ordinarily you are unaware of the atmosphere pressing down on you. But sometimes your ears may make you conscious of outside pressure changes. In each ear you have a eustachian tube. Eustachian tubes are passages that connect the inside of the ear to your throat. They regulate the flow of air to the ears. While the air surrounding you pushes against your body, the air inside your ears presses outward with the same intensity.

Sometimes your ears can't adjust quickly enough to sudden changes in pressure. They feel clogged, and sounds become muffled. You may even feel a sharp pain. This can happen when riding in an elevator, or when you gain or drop in altitude in a car or plane. Swallowing or yawning can help "pop" your ears by adjusting the pressure inside your ear to the air pressure outside, allowing you to hear normally again.

Temperature affects air pressure. If air is cooled, the molecules move more slowly and become more closely spaced. Cold air contains more molecules and more mass than warm air of the same volume, so it pushes with more pressure. If the air is warmed, the molecules move faster and spread farther apart. Warm air has fewer molecules and less mass than the same volume of cold air. It also exerts less pressure.

Differences in pressure and temperature create wind—air on the move. The slighter the difference, the lighter the breeze. You can see wind create waves on a lake, rustle leaves on a tree, and lift kites into the air. Vast differences in pressure and temperature create winds of titanic proportion—tornadoes strong enough to uproot trees and lift homes from their foundations.

You don't need to be a meteorologist to measure the wind. You can use a wind scale developed in 1805 by a British admiral, Sir Francis Beaufort. (See chart on page 35.)

Whatever their strength, winds can be blamed on the sun. Although the sun is about 93 million miles from the Earth, it is the heat engine that drives our planet's winds. Rays of sunlight hit the Earth's surface, heating the land and sea, fields and forests, and buildings and other human constructions. In turn, these objects radiate some of their heat, warming the air close above them.

But the sun does not heat the Earth evenly. Some parts of the Earth's surface receive more energy than others. Sunlight reaches only half the planet at a time—the side facing the sun. The other half, the side facing away from the sun, is in darkness and loses heat.

Differences between land and water affect air temperature, too. Land heats up more quickly than water and cools down faster. As a result, in summer the air over the ocean is usually cooler than the air over the adjacent land. In winter it is the opposite.

THE BEAUFORT SCALE

Beaufort Number	Wind speed	Description	Observations
0	under 1 mph (under 1 knot)	calm	smoke rises straight up
1	1–3 mph (1–3 knots)	light breeze	drift of smoke shows wind direction
2	4–7 mph (4–6 knots)	slight breeze	leaves rustle; wind felt on face
3	8–12 mph (7–10 knots)	gentle breeze	leaves and twigs in constant motion
4	13–18 mph (11–16 knots)	moderate breeze	small branches move; dust and loose paper are moved
5	19–24 mph (17–21 knots)	fresh breeze	small trees sway
6	25–31 mph (22–27 knots)	strong breeze	large branches move
7	32–38 mph (28–33 knots)	moderate gale	whole trees sway
8	39–46 mph (34–40 knots)	fresh gale	twigs snap off trees
9	47–54 mph (41–47 knots)	strong gale	branches break; slight damage to buildings
10	55–63 mph (48–55 knots)	whole gale	trees uprooted; moderate building damage
11	64–72 mph (56–63 knots)	storm	widespread damage
12	73 mph and over (64+ knots)	hurricane force	extreme damage

If you look carefully at a globe you will notice that the globe is mounted at an angle on its stand. This angle represents the amount that the Earth tilts on its axis. The Earth's tilted axis also contributes to the heating imbalance. The sun's rays beat down most directly near the equator, soaking the region with light and heat energy. Here you find the tropics, a wide band centering on the equator. Tropical regions are known for their hot temperatures.

The North and South Poles, on the other hand, are famous for their cold. The sun never shines directly overhead at the poles. It hovers low in the sky, even at noon in summer. Its rays strike the surface at a slant, spreading the heat and light over a large area.

This heat imbalance puts the air in motion. Day and night, warm air expands, and becomes lighter. It rises as a bubble over the sun-warmed surface of the planet. Cooler, heavier air sinks down to replace it. As air moves from places where pressure is high toward places where pressure is low—whoosh!—wind results.

You can check out for yourself the difference in the movement of warm air and cold air. Open the door to a freezer. Place your hand above the open door and then below it. You should notice that the cold air sinks but doesn't rise. Place your hand over a steaming hot cup of tea or cocoa. You'll notice that the hot air rises.

SNOWSTORMS AND CHANGING WEATHER

SLAVEY

ALASKA AND CANADA

When the world was young and people had not yet appeared, birds, fish, and four-legged animals peacefully shared the Earth. They spoke the same language, formed friendships, and even married. Some of them had special powers, like Fox, who was especially clever and sly, and Lynx, who could change himself into other shapes.

One winter night, thick clouds gathered on the horizon and snow started to fall. The snow fell throughout the next day and week, and the following month and year. Three years passed and still the snow kept falling. During that time the sun never came out. Not so

much as a single ray of sunshine broke through the clouds. As a result, all the animals were cold and running out of food because nothing could grow.

A grand council was called to find out what had caused this catastrophe. Everyone attended the meeting except the bears. The other animals couldn't recall seeing any bears in the three years since the trouble began, and they thought this was strange. Nonetheless, they had more important things to worry about.

The animals decided that something in the Upper World was preventing the sun from shining. So they set out on an expedition to explore it. Finding the opening to the Upper World was not simple. The animals searched far and wide with no success. Finally a small group found a door in the sky. They climbed through it and began to explore this new place.

To their surprise, they found that the Upper World was remarkably similar to their own. It had forests and meadows, rivers and streams. Eventually they stumbled upon a small tepee nestled on the shore of a large blue lake. They poked their heads inside the tepee and found two young bear cubs.

"Where is your mother?" asked the explorers.

"She is hunting," the cubs replied.

The explorers noticed four large, round bags inside the tepee.

Lynx pointed to the first bag. "What is in this?" he asked.

"Rain," replied the cubs.

Mouse pointed to the second bag. "What is in that one?" he asked.

"Wind," said the cubs.

"This one?" asked Fox, pointing to the third.

"Fog."

"And the last bag?" asked Wolf.

The two cubs looked at each other, and shook their heads. "We can't tell you," they replied. "Our mother said it was a secret, and we are not allowed to tell anybody."

"Don't worry," said Fox. "We will never let your mother know that you told us."

"Okay," said the cubs. "The sun is in that bag."

The explorers now had the information they sought, so they politely said good-bye to the little bears and left the tepee.

On his way out, Fox said to the cubs, "Be on the lookout for any deer, which might be grazing on the far side of the lake."

The animals disappeared into the woods and held a council. Fox laid out his plan. Lynx would change himself into a deer and walk along the far side of the lake. This would catch the attention of the little bears. Meanwhile, Mouse would creep into Mother Bear's canoe and gnaw a deep gash in the handle of the paddle. The other animals were to hide near the tepee.

And so it went. Lynx changed himself into a deer and pretended to graze along the opposite shore. The young bears spied him and excitedly pointed him out to their mother when she returned home.

Mother Bear, anticipating a scrumptious meal of deer meat for herself and her children, jumped into the canoe. As she paddled across the water, "Deer" pretended not to see her. He wanted to lure the bear closer. Just as she drew near the shore, he bolted.

In an attempt to catch up with him, Mother Bear paddled furiously. But her powerful strokes put too much stress on the paddle. It broke in two where Mouse had gnawed it. Mother Bear lost her balance and tumbled into the water. Watching from the lakefront, the two little cubs began jumping up and down, urging their mother to swim quickly to shore to catch the deer.

During the commotion, the other animals raced into the tepee and took the bag containing the sun. The bag was extremely heavy, and so the animals took turns dragging it toward the doorway to their own world.

Lynx soon caught up to them. He had already changed back into his true form. "Quick!" he shouted. "Mother Bear will be after us the moment she discovers that we have taken the sun."

But the going was slow because the bag was so heavy and the animals tired easily. Before long, Mother Bear was hot on their trail. She caught up to them just as the animals squeezed through the door, pulling the heavy sack through with them. Defeated, Mother Bear gave a loud growl and then stormed home to have a long talk with her cubs.

Victorious, the other animals gleefully tore open the bag. The sun popped out and resumed its proper place in the sky, radiating light and warmth on the land. At last the long winter faded, and the sounds of rejoicing could be heard throughout the world.

〓〓〓

If you think of the sky as one big battleground with air masses as armies, you can better understand Earth's changing weather. An air mass is a humongous air bubble, often covering millions of square miles. An air mass forms when air settles over the same region for a long period.

In the tropics, the hot and wet conditions over the oceans produce warm, moist air masses that rise and drift toward the poles. At the poles the frigid, dry conditions over ice sheets produce cold, dry air masses that sink and migrate toward the equator. There are also warm, dry air masses that arise over land in tropical areas, and cold, moist air masses that develop over polar oceans.

Whenever an air mass moves, it can ram into an air mass already squatting over a patch of land. The place where the two different air masses collide is called a front. A front is highlighted by turbulent weather.

If a cold air mass bullies its way in, its leading edge is called a cold front. Usually, when a cold front pushes through, lofty storm clouds build up rapidly. A heavy rain or snowstorm may dump a lot of moisture on the ground. And then within a few hours the skies clear and cooler air moves in.

If a warm air mass meanders in, its leading edge is referred to as a warm front. It tends to move slower than a cold front and brings less dramatic changes. Typically, a thick layer of clouds precedes a warm front. As the front approaches, a steady but gentle rain or snow falls, followed by a few warm, humid, mostly clear days.

SEASONS

ACOMA

SOUTHWEST

Long ago the chief of the Acoma people had a beautiful daughter named Co-Chin-ne-na-ko, who was called Co-Chin. Co-Chin lived with her family in a pueblo carved into a high cliff in the southwestern desert. Co-Chin's beauty and warmth captured the heart of every young man in the village. Although she could have her choice, she desired none of them.

One day a tall, rugged stranger climbed the steep stone ladder to the pueblo. Pure white crystals covered his clothing and glistened as he moved. Though he appeared serious and unsmiling, his face was strong and handsome.

Co-Chin's eyes followed the stranger as he strode confidently into the village. Briefly he glanced her way as she filled her water jar at the spring. Moments later he was gone.

Soon Co-Chin learned that the stranger's name was Shakok, the Spirit of Winter. They began to see each other, and after a short courtship she married him. Perhaps if Co-Chin had known him longer before agreeing to be his wife, great hardship could have been avoided. For once Shakok came to live with Co-Chin and her people, the seasons grew colder. Corn withered on the stalk. Snow and ice lingered longer on the ground. Water froze in the springs.

Early each morning Shakok left the pueblo and hurried to his home in the far north. There he played all day with the North Wind, churning out snow, hail, sleet, and an occasional blizzard. Each evening he returned, frost-covered, and chilled the desert around him. Co-Chin discovered that Shakok's heart was as cold as the frozen air he brought with him. Nothing she did could warm his blustery nature.

In the bitter cold brought on by Shakok, no crops could grow. The Acoma people were hungry and grew desperate. To hold off starvation, they harvested cactus leaves, roasting them first to burn off their sharp thorns.

One day while roasting cactus leaves, Co-Chin was approached by another handsome stranger. He wore a yellow shirt woven from corn silk, and green pants sewn from the moss that covers rocks in springs and ponds. Flashing a smile as warm as sunshine, the stranger asked Co-Chin what she was doing. Co-Chin explained the plight of her people and how they would soon starve if the frigid weather continued.

The young man listened intently. When Co-Chin finished her sad tale, he handed her an ear of corn. "Eat this!" he commanded. "And wait here while I fetch a bundle for you to take home."

He raced off toward the south and quickly disappeared from sight. Co-Chin barely had time to finish eating before he reappeared with an armload of corn.

"Where did you find this?" asked an astonished Co-Chin. "Does it grow nearby?"

"It comes from my home far to the south, where the sun shines every day and corn grows all year round," he replied.

"I would love to see your home," said Co-Chin. "Please take me with you."

"I cannot do that. Your husband, the Spirit of Winter, would be furious," replied the young man.

"Our love is dead," Co-Chin replied. "He is cold-hearted and has no feeling for me or my people. Since he settled here no crops can grow, no flowers can blossom."

"Take the corn home to your family," said the young man. "Then meet me here tomorrow, and I will bring you another load." With that, he turned and headed south.

When Co-Chin arrived home, her parents were shocked to see corn instead of cactus leaves. She told them of the warm young man and his generous offer to provide more corn.

"He is Miochin," said her father.

"Yes," agreed her mother. "He must be Miochin, the Spirit of Summer. Invite him home with you tomorrow."

The next day, Co-Chin met the young man at the prearranged spot, and she asked him his name. He confessed that he was Miochin, the Spirit of Summer. This time he had brought with him enough corn to feed the entire village. Together Co-Chin and Miochin carried the bundles to the pueblo. As they walked, clear skies and warm sunshine followed them. The frozen springs began to thaw.

Co-Chin's parents welcomed Miochin into their home, and he was still there when Shakok returned from the north. As the Spirit of Winter approached the village, he knew instantly that Miochin was present and that he had captured Co-Chin's heart.

With the voice of the coldest wind, Shakok called out, "Miochin, come out here!"

Dark clouds swirled overhead, and sleet and hail pelted down from the sky. The frost clinging to Shakok's shirt and pants grew into long, thick icicles.

Miochin emerged from Co-Chin's home, bringing a ray of sunshine.

"I will destroy you!" bellowed Shakok.

"No, I will destroy you!" said Miochin. Radiating the heat of a perfect summer day, he advanced toward his foe. Instantly the sleet and hail were reduced to a light sprinkle of rain, and the icicles began to melt.

"We will see who is more powerful," shouted Shakok. "But not today. In four days we will meet again and the winner will take Co-Chin." With that, Shakok stormed off to the north.

The wind howled and rattled the walls of the houses in the pueblo. But inside, the people stayed safe and warm because Miochin remained with them.

The following day Miochin returned to his home to prepare for battle. First he summoned his friend Yat-Moot, who lived in the west. Next he requested the help of all the birds, insects, and four-legged animals that lived in the warm lands. Then he assigned Bat to be his advance guard, for Bat's skin was tough and would be able to withstand the assault of Shakok's sleet and hail.

When Yat-Moot arrived the day before the battle, he kindled huge bonfires. Then he heated thin, flat stones for Miochin to use in the fight. These flat stones would produce a warm South Wind, Miochin's most potent weapon.

Meanwhile, in the north, Shakok prepared by asking all the birds and four-legged animals of the cold lands to aid him. He appointed Magpie to serve as his shield and advance guard.

On the morning of the conflict, the people of Acoma watched the two enemies advancing toward their village. From the north, towering storm clouds heavy with snow, sleet, and hail conveyed Shakok to the battleground. From the south, billowing clouds of steam and smoke from Yat-Moot's fire filled the sky and delivered Miochin.

Jagged bolts of lightning inside Shakok's clouds singed the fur and feathers of the animals accompanying him. To this day the creatures of the north have some white coloring.

The thick smoke from Yat-Moot's fire blackened the animals who came with Miochin. Even now animals living in the south have brown or black coloring.

At last the warriors reached the pueblo. In a blinding storm of sleet and ice, Shakok created a bitter wind that froze all the waters. But Miochin called upon the South Wind, and the warm wind thawed the ice.

Shakok then whipped up a blizzard that covered the entire world in a thick coating of snow. Miochin again called the South Wind, and the warm wind melted the snow.

Finally Shakok caused great icicles to rain down until they buried everything in the world. Once more Miochin summoned the warm South Wind, and the icicles quickly vanished.

At last Shakok admitted defeat and asked for a truce. Miochin agreed. At once the winds died down and the sky cleared. Co-Chin was free to go with Miochin.

In the harmony of the moment, the Spirit of Summer offered to share the land with the Spirit of Winter. Shakok would prevail for half of every year, and Miochin would rule for the other half. Since the great battle of the spirits, the world experiences six months of cold and six months of warmth annually.

Like a giant top, the Earth spins on its axis, an imaginary line through its center. The North Pole and the South Pole straddle the ends of the axis. About every 24 hours, the Earth completes one full turn. Although you cannot feel the planet rotating, you can see its effects. The Earth's rotation causes day and night. No matter where you live on our world, the sun appears to rise in the eastern sky each morning because the Earth twirls on its axis in a west-to-east direction.

Most places on the planet receive sunlight for some part of each day. But the number of daylight hours changes throughout the year. In spring and summer, the sun rises earlier and sets later than in winter and fall. Each day still has 24 hours, but in spring and summer there are more hours of daylight than darkness. With the additional hours of sunlight, the air temperature is warmer.

The change in the number of daylight hours during a day is caused by the tilt of the Earth's axis as it orbits the sun. The tilt is significant enough to create seasons. On the first day of summer in the Northern Hemisphere, the North Pole leans toward the sun. North America receives more hours of daylight, the sun's rays strike more directly, and the weather is warmer.

At the same time, the South Pole is pointed away from the sun. In Australia, a continent in the Southern Hemisphere, the number of daylight hours are fewer, rays of sunlight strike the surface at a greater slant, and the weather is colder. So while you are sweltering in the heat of summer in North America, somewhere in Australia kids are shivering in the cold! When the Earth's orbit around the sun carries it to the position where the North Pole tips away from the sun, winter returns to North America, and summer begins in Australia.

In the wind chapter you learned that the equator receives far more solar energy than the poles. Consequently, the air above the equator is scorching hot in comparison to the icy air above the poles. In the tropics, the area around the equator, there are two main seasons—wet and dry.

The poles have only one season—cold. The air remains frigid throughout the year with little variation in temperature. For example, during December and January, the sunniest months at the South Pole, the warmest temperature ever recorded was 8°F. The average summer temperature there is minus 15°F. Antarctica holds the record for the coldest winter temperature ever recorded—an astounding minus 129°F in 1983.

The regions between the poles and the tropics are called the temperate zones. Temperate zones have four distinct seasons: spring, summer, fall, and winter.

If the Earth had no tilt, there would be twelve hours of daylight and twelve hours of darkness each day of the year everywhere. The slant of the sun's rays would remain the same for each particular location on the planet, and there would be no seasonal variation anywhere.

INDIAN SUMMER

PENOBSCOT

MAINE

Long ago when spirits still spoke to human beings, there lived an old man named Zimo. He resided in a Penobscot village in what is now Maine. Like his neighbors, Zimo planted a vegetable crop each summer so he would have food for the winter. But one year Zimo fell ill at the start of planting season. He was too weak to tend his garden.

Each day the old man thought his strength would come back, but the entire summer passed before he was strong enough to leave his sick bed. By now it was fall. The air had turned crisp and cold, and low gray clouds filled the sky. The other people in Zimo's village had already harvested and dried their vegetables for the long months ahead. They had provisions for winter, but Zimo had none.

Zimo knew that without food he could not survive the harsh winter. So he went to the Creator for help.

"I was ill throughout the summer," he said. "I could not plant my vegetables and now I have no provisions for winter. What can I do?"

"Go and plant your seeds now," replied the Creator. "Your crop will grow immediately."

Zimo returned home and set to work in his garden. First he prepared the soil. Then he planted corn, squash, beans, and pumpkins, and fertilized them with fish heads. And as the Creator promised, the seeds sprouted immediately.

The weather turned warm and the skies cleared. It felt more like summer than late fall. But the leaves on the trees had already turned beautiful shades of red, yellow, and orange, a sign that winter was not far off.

Zimo watered the tiny plants and weeded the garden. By the end of the second day the plants had blossomed, and tiny vegetables began to form. Each day after that the vegetables grew larger and larger. Within seven days the corn, beans, squash, and even the pumpkins were ready for picking. Just as the Creator had promised, Zimo now had a bountiful harvest. He would have ample food to see him through the winter.

As quickly as the warm weather arrived, it departed. The days became chilly and the nights even colder. Every morning a thin layer of frost glazed the countryside. Winter closed in.

The Penobscots called that sudden warm spell in autumn "person's summer." They remembered its brief, renewing properties. Nowadays, when summer's warmth returns in fall, we call it "Indian Summer."

Usually each autumn after a killing frost—a freezing cold night that destroys unharvested fruits and vegetables—there is a spell of unseasonably warm, dry, hazy weather. These spells of Indian Summer generally last about five days and may occur more than once in a season. Some years they do not appear at all.

The origin of the term Indian Summer has been lost to history. However, the term has been in use since at least the late 1700s. One explanation for it relates to the way Native Americans in colonial times took advantage of the summerlike weather to increase their stores of animal meat before the onslaught of winter.

According to this account, the pleasant weather and the haziness of the air encouraged game animals to wander in the open. Native American hunters were able to make their kills more readily than on clear days. The more meat the hunters were able to stockpile, the more likely they and their families would survive the cold, barren season to come.

Indian Summer arrives in autumn after the leaves have begun to turn color and a spate of crisp, cool weather has frosted the landscape. The mild weather is ushered in by winds from the south or southwest that carry a large mass of warm, tropical air.

CLOUDS AND RAIN

PUEBLO

SOUTHWEST

In days long gone in the great expanse of the Southwest lived a young man called Kahp-too-óo-yoo, the Cornstalk Young Man. A skilled hunter and unfailing with his bow, Kahp-too-óo-yoo never returned empty-handed from the chase. A bold warrior, too, Kahp-too-óo-yoo was feared and respected by his enemies from other tribes. However, of all his abilities, none was as amazing as his power with the clouds, for the Creator had made him a wizard.

Whenever he wished, Kahp-too-óo-yoo could wrench moisture from the clouds. He could make the drops drizzle gently to the ground. Or he could force them to pound heavily in great downpours. No one else could coax rain from the sky, not even his parents or two sisters.

Despite his gift, Kahp-too-óo-yoo tried to live a normal life. He spent many of his days away from his village with a friend he had known since childhood. Together the young men competed in races, gathered wood in the mountains, and hunted wild game. The two seemed inseparable. But the friend was a rogue and not a true friend. Inside him resided an evil spirit.

One day when the morning mists were still entwined in the treetops, the two men startled a small deer herd. Kahp-too-óo-yoo chased the ones that fled up a mountain trail. The rogue pursued the part of the herd that retreated alongside a wending stream.

Kahp-too-óo-yoo's aim with the arrow was true, and he brought down a large deer. Lugging his kill on his back, he retraced his steps to the place where he and his companion had parted. The friend returned shortly, exhausted and empty-handed. When he saw the deer, jealousy possessed him. But Kahp-too-óo-yoo was oblivious to the envy.

"Let us share the deer as brothers," said Kahp-too-óo-yoo. "Take part of it home as though you felled it with your own arrow."

"I cannot accept it," replied the other, cold as ice.

When the two men reached Kahp-too-óo-yoo's home, his sisters saw the deer and praised their brother's hunting skills. A dark shadow crossed the friend's face, and he headed to his own home filled with bitterness.

When the young men next returned to the mountain, the same thing happened. And it occurred the following time, and the time after that. Kahp-too-óo-yoo always succeeded in the hunt, and his companion always failed. Each time Kahp-too-óo-yoo offered to share the deer as brothers, and the rogue always refused.

With each failure the rogue grew more and more envious. Finally, he said, "Kahp-too-óo-yoo, prove to me that you are honestly my friend, because I don't believe you are. A true friend would not embarrass me in the hunt the way you do."

"I will gladly prove my friendship," replied Kahp-too-óo-yoo. He was blind to the insult of the request.

"Then let's play a game together," said the rogue, "the gallo race."

"But that is played on horseback with a live chicken! We have neither a horse nor a chicken!" said Kahp-too-óo-yoo.

The rogue led him deep into the heart of the forest, where sunshine never penetrated. There he picked up a large stone and said, "Since we don't have a chicken, we can use this stone." He then pointed to a misshapen pine tree with a low limb, and threw the stone beneath it. "Instead of a horse we will use this tree limb." He mounted the limb as though it were a horse. While "riding" it he bent down and scooped up the "chicken."

When he was done, it was Kahp-too-óo-yoo's turn. No sooner had Kahp-too-óo-yoo plunked down on the branch than his companion cast a spell upon the tree. The pine shot straight up to the sky, taking Kahp-too-óo-yoo with it. The traitor then seized Kahp-too-óo-yoo's deer and returned to the village.

By this time the day was nearly done, and long shadows stretched across the land. Kahp-too-óo-yoo's sisters had grown worried. When they saw the rogue enter the village alone, they raced up to him and asked, "Where is Kahp-too-óo-yoo?"

"I have not seen him," replied the traitor. "We went in different directions and he did not return to our meeting place."

The rogue then offered the deer to the sisters. They declined and trudged home with heavy hearts. As the hours passed, their worry changed to numbing fear.

Days slipped by and then weeks and months with no sign of Kahp-too-óo-yoo. His parents and sisters mourned him, and the villagers shared in their loss.

The springs dried up. The crops shriveled in the fields. The dogs lay listless in the shade. People walked around like weary shadows. For without Kahp-too-óo-yoo, no rain could fall. Only Kahp-too-óo-yoo had the power to squeeze water from the clouds and relieve the aching earth.

When their friends and neighbors began to die, Kahp-too-óo-yoo's father said to his daughters, "We must search for your brother."

The father traveled to the south, the mother to the east, one sister to the north, and the other to the west. They wandered over rugged hills and through deep canyons, calling out Kahp-too-óo-yoo's name, looking for traces of his footprints. Now and then they would pause to listen. But they heard only the sound of their own hard breathing.

Finally, the sister who traveled north caught the strains of a faint song. She stopped to focus in on the sound and heard a man singing about his father, who was called Old Black Cane, and his mother, who was known as Corn Woman.

And she knew that this was her brother's song because their parents were named Old Black Cane and Corn Woman. So she ran, shouting for her sister. When the younger sister joined her, she, too, listened to the song, and agreed. This was Kahp-too-óo-yoo's song. They quickly found their parents, and together the four followed the strains of the music. It led them to the sky-scraping pine.

On the ground by the tree lay Kahp-too-óo-yoo's bow and arrows. But there was no sign of him. His parents and sisters called for him again and again, until their throats were so strained that no sounds would come from them. But Kahp-too-óo-yoo was too high up to hear their voices. Disheartened, the family plodded home.

A short while later, Little Black Ant came upon the bewitched pine tree and scaled it. At the top he was shocked to discover Kahp-too-óo-yoo in his sky-high prison.

"Man with the power of the clouds," said Little Black Ant, "why do you sit up here while your people are dying of thirst below?"

Kahp-too-óo-yoo told Little Black Ant his sad tale of trickery and betrayal. Then he added, "Soon I will no longer be. I am dying from hunger."

"I will help you," promised Little Black Ant.

Little Black Ant raced down the tree and summoned the ant nation. Within hours all the little black ants and all the big red ants gathered at the base of the pine. There, they decided that the big red ants would tackle the bottom of the tree and the little black ants would work on the top.

Before they started, Little Black Ant gave Kahp-too-óo-yoo an acorn filled with a mix of cornmeal, honey, and water. "Eat this," he said.

Kahp-too-óo-yoo saw how little food the acorn held. *I'm starving*, he thought. *This little morsel of food won't be enough.*

Little Black Ant read his thoughts. "This little bit is sufficient," he said. "There will even be some left over."

So Kahp-too-óo-yoo ate and ate until he could eat no more. Yet food still remained in the acorn.

"Now close your eyes," instructed Little Black Ant.

Kahp-too-óo-yoo shut his eyes, and the ants commenced their rescue. The little black ants placed their feet against the sky and pushed down on the tree with all their strength. The big red ants pulled with all their might from below. Together they drove the pine tree a quarter of its length into the ground.

Kahp-too-óo-yoo opened his eyes but could see only blue sky.

"Close your eyes again," ordered Little Black Ant.

For a second time, the little black ants pushed from above, and the big red ants pulled from below. The tree sank another quarter of its length below the surface.

Kahp-too-óo-yoo opened his eyes. He saw the world and how brown it had become.

Kahp-too-óo-yoo closed his eyes again. And for a third time the little black ants pushed from above, and the big red ants pulled from below. The tree was driven another quarter of its length deeper.

When Kahp-too-óo-yoo opened his eyes, he saw his little village with its dried-out fields and dying inhabitants. Sadness flooded over him and tears welled up.

Kahp-too-óo-yoo shut his eyes yet again. For the final time, the mighty ants pushed and pulled. They forced the pine tree completely into the soil. Kahp-too-óo-yoo plopped gently to the ground. In gratitude, he killed a deer and distributed it among the ants.

Kahp-too-óo-yoo made his way home, singing a quiet song. And as he sang, tufts of puffy white clouds floated overhead, and a gentle rain fell from the sky. Wherever he walked the brown, thirsty plants turned lush and green.

When he arrived home, his astonished sisters rushed out to greet him, but his parents were too weak to rise.

"Sisters," Kahp-too-óo-yoo said, "prepare a meal for the family to eat."

"How can we?" they answered. "The storeroom is empty and our crops have all died."

"Look in the storeroom," he answered.

Kahp-too-óo-yoo's magical powers surprised his sisters. For when they entered the storeroom they found it brimming with corn. Soon every storeroom in the village was bursting with wheat and corn.

All the villagers except one sang and danced to celebrate the return of Kahp-too-óo-yoo. The rogue remained alone in his house. When his friends and family learned of his treachery, they shunned him and he died of shame.

Have you ever watched clouds float across the sky? Did you notice that their shapes constantly change? Clouds provide powerful clues to what is happening in the atmosphere and can be used to predict approaching weather.

Where do clouds come from? Each day energy from the sun evaporates enormous amounts of water from Earth's oceans, lakes, rivers, and land, turning liquid water into gaseous water vapor. Warm, dry air sops up the water vapor like an invisible sponge. The warm air, now full of moisture, bubbles up into the atmosphere. As the air rises, it cools.

You can't see water vapor in the air, but you can force it to come out. Take a plastic glass and place four ice cubes in it. Fill the glass three-fourths full with lemonade or any other cold drink. Wipe the outside of the glass to make sure it is dry. Wait a minute and then examine the outside of the glass. You should notice moisture collecting on it. Note also that the moisture does not have any color, so it could not have come from inside the glass.

The glass cooled the air beside it. Cool air does not hold as much moisture as warm air. When air cools enough, the water vapor in it reaches its dewpoint. It begins to condense and change into water droplets. If the air temperature is below freezing, ice crystals form instead of droplets. When condensation takes place high in the sky, water condenses on dust and other bits of matter, and clouds are born. When it occurs near the ground, fog forms.

Clouds are named for their shape and altitude. You'll find cirrus clouds high in the sky. These wispy clouds are made of ice crystals. Generally they form in fair weather, but they often signal the approach of nasty weather.

On overcast days, stratus clouds blanket the sky in a thick layer. They generally hang low in the sky, blocking the sun. They herald the arrival of a soft, steady rainfall or snow.

Fluffy white clouds that scoot across the sky are called cumulus clouds. They appear in fair weather and can form at various altitudes. However, under certain conditions these peaceful-looking clouds can mutate into colossal thunderheads, and even produce tornadoes.

Updrafts—strong upward currents of air—keep clouds afloat. If the water droplets inside the cloud combine to produce large drops, they may become too heavy for the updrafts to support. The drops fall as rain. If rain falls through a thick layer of freezing-cold air, the drops turn into pellets of ice called sleet.

If the temperature of a cloud is below freezing, ice crystals appear instead of drops. The crystals clump together and fall as snowflakes. If the snowflakes pass through a layer of warm air, they may melt and change into rain.

Hailstones are lumps of ice that form only in thunderclouds. A hailstone starts as a big raindrop. Strong updrafts inside the cloud whisk the drop upward into very cold air. The raindrop freezes and falls back down to warmer levels in the cloud where it is coated with water. Winds thrust it upward again where it freezes. Each time this happens the hailstone grows larger, adding layers like an onion. This process repeats itself until the hailstone becomes so heavy that the wind can't push it upward again. It plunks to the ground. The largest known hailstone weighed about 2 pounds. It fell during a hailstorm over Bangladesh in 1986 that took the lives of 92 people.

THUNDER, LIGHTNING, AND TORNADOES

LAKOTA SIOUX

PLAINS

The warriors of thunder and lightning dwell in stormy skies. Mounted on giant white horses, they wildly ride the billowing black clouds. Their fists clasp lightning sticks, which light up the sky. The hoofs of their galloping horses create the crashes of thunder heard below.

Since the early days the people of the plains had become accustomed to the occasional clatter above. They knew that sometimes a lightning stick would slip from a warrior's hand and strike a tree or even a tepee. However, most of the time when black clouds churned overhead, the mounted warriors of thunder and lightning dashed madly about without harming anyone or anything beneath them. The people were grateful for the storms because they brought rains that revived the plants and refreshed the streams.

But one summer morning a hunting party left their camp near the Black Hills of South Dakota in search of buffalo. Throughout the day the sun beat down, turning the air hot and heavy. Thick dark clouds rolled in from the west, coloring the sky a deep purple. On the ground, wind gusts stirred up the dust.

The men came upon a buffalo herd but decided to wait out the advancing storm before beginning the hunt. An immense thundercloud soon filled the horizon, and lightning flickered across the sky. Accustomed to storms, the men sensed unusual danger in this one. Their apprehension grew deeper when they noticed part of the cloud dipping menacingly close to the ground.

Inside the billowing mass, the thunder and lightning warriors raced crazily back and forth on their steeds. Deafening booms from the trampling hoofs shook the air and rattled the ground. Lightning sticks created blinding flashes of light shaped like tree roots, capable of striking many objects at one time.

Uneasy, the buffalo crowded together in a tight group. Glowing blue sparks of light appeared on the tips of their horns. Suddenly the skies blackened, the wind shrieked, and great drops of rain pounded down. The frightened animals snorted and pawed the ground.

Before the buffalo could stampede, the cloud swooped down upon them. The warriors astride their giant horses charged the herd. The panicked buffalo tried to flee, but the warriors were too fast. As the hunters on the ground watched in terror, the sky warriors began to strike the animals dead with their powerful lightning sticks. The wind swirled and roared, forming a gigantic cone that hurtled the buffalo up into the air.

As quickly as it appeared, the black cloud vanished. Soon the skies cleared and the sun returned. The bodies of dead buffalo littered the countryside, and in the moist soil were hoofprints left behind by the giant horses. Shaken, the hunters returned home, amazed to be alive.

Lightning will strike our planet nearly 9 million times within the next 24 hours. That breaks down to roughly 100 zaps of lightning per second. In the United States, Florida has the distinction of being the state with the most lightning.

Lightning usually forms in towering thunderclouds 15,000 to 20,000 feet above the ground. Even though thunderclouds are enormous, the cause of lightning is extraordinarily small.

Like all matter, the water droplets and ice crystals in a thundercloud are made of atoms. You probably know that each atom consists of protons, neutrons, and electrons. A proton has a positive charge, and a neutron has no charge. Together, they make up the nucleus, or center, of the atom. The nucleus has a positive charge. Electrons whirl around the nucleus. They have a negative charge.

Usually, the number of electrons in an atom equals the number of protons. Thus the positive charges and the negative charges are balanced and the atom has no charge. However, collisions with other atoms can upset the balance. Electrons can be lost or gained.

You can upset the balance of electrons in your hair by rubbing your head with a balloon. Your hair, which started with an equal number of electrons and protons, loses electrons to the balloon. Your hair now has more protons than electrons. It carries a positive charge. The balloon has more electrons, so it carries a negative charge.

If the day is dry and you rub the balloon on your head in a dark room, you may see little flashes of light in a mirror and hear crackling sounds. The electrons that piled up on the balloon jumped back onto your hair, creating a tiny spark of electricity.

Something similar happens in a thundercloud, only on a much grander scale. Strong updrafts hurl ice crystals and water droplets up and down within the clouds. Some of the ice crystals and water droplets get pulled apart, and they develop electrical charges. The top of the cloud becomes positively charged, while the bottom of the cloud develops a negative charge.

Eventually the charges build up so much that the negative ones jump toward the positive, creating a streak of lightning. The gigantic spark may leap from one part of a cloud to another or from cloud to cloud. If enough electrical attraction exists between the cloud and positive charges on the ground, lightning darts to the Earth's surface.

Five times hotter than the surface of the sun, a lightning bolt superheats the air around it and causes the air to expand in a sound wave. You hear the sound wave as the crackle or boom of thunder. Because light travels faster than sound, there is usually a delay between the time you see lightning flash and hear its thunder. If you count the seconds that elapse between the flash and the rumble, and divide by five, you can calculate your distance in miles from the lightning.

Perhaps the eeriest display of electrical phenomena is Saint Elmo's fire, the strange blue glow that appeared on the horn tips of the buffalo in the preceding legend. Saint Elmo's fire is a lightning bolt that fizzled. It occurs when the damp air next to the tip of an object develops a positive charge. Electrons from the surrounding air leap toward the positive charge, causing a steady blue glow in the air. The attraction between the opposite charges is not great enough to generate a lightning flash. Saint Elmo's fire has been spotted on church steeples, ship masts, and airplane wings, as well as on the horns of cattle and buffalo. It is harmless. Ordinary lightning, however, is usually deadly.

TORNADOES

Under the right conditions severe thunderstorms can give birth to tornadoes. Tornadoes are swirling funnels of air that can drop down from thunderheads. They arise in the violent clashes of air masses with different pressures: usually a cold, heavy air mass from the poles slams into a light, warm air mass from the tropics.

At the storm front, powerful winds develop as warm air soars upward while cool air swooshes down to take its place. A thin line of thunderstorms begins to brew. Deafening thunderclaps reverberate through the air. Lightning slashes the sky. Rain and hail rocket downward.

At the storm's peak, the inrushing air spirals at tremendous speed around a center of low pressure. A funnel appears at the base of the cloud. Like a giant straw, it can slurp up nearly everything beneath it, even a herd of buffalo. Whirling soil and debris trapped in the tornado give the funnel its black coloring.

The life span of the average tornado is only a few minutes. It measures 150 feet across, careens across the land at a speed of 30 miles per hour, and cuts a swath of destruction about 2 miles long. However, it is the long-lived, but fortunately rare, monster tornadoes that make the headlines. Traveling at 60 miles per hour, they may persist up to three hours or so with wind speeds exceeding 300 miles per hour. They may cut a path more than a mile wide and more than 60 miles long.

The most lethal tornado in history ripped through three states in March 1925. Called the Tri-State Tornado, it originated in eastern Missouri, whipped across southern Illinois, and died out in Indiana, a journey of 219 miles. During its 3½-hour dance of terror, the twister wrenched trees from the ground, tore houses from their foundations, and killed 689 people.

DROUGHT AND CLIMATE

PAPAGO

SOUTHWEST

Long ago during the hottest part of each summer, the water holes dried up in the southwest. When this happened the Desert People ran out of water. So each year they moved from their villages in the valley to the foothills of the neighboring mountains. They camped in the shadow of the mountains, where water was plentiful and enough cactus fruit grew for the women to gather and turn into wine and preserves.

One day while the women were cooking and most of the men were tending their crops, four wise old men climbed the steep mountainside. After an ascent of an hour or so they reached their favorite destination, a rocky ledge with a panoramic view of the valley below. From their perch the men saw the lush green fields of corn, beans, wheat, and pumpkins that filled the valley from side to side.

"It is a pity that the valley is so small," said one of the wise men. "If it were larger we could plant more fields and grow more food for our people."

"Perhaps we could ask the Great Spirit to help us push back the mountains to make more room," suggested another of the wise men.

The four men pondered this for a while and decided to seek the help of the Great Spirit. They climbed the rest of the way up the steep mountain to the very top, where the cave of the Great Spirit was located. There, the wise old men spoke at length with the Great Spirit, and he explained precisely what they must do to widen the valley.

When the men returned to their camp in the foothills of the mountain, they told the people to assemble and prepare a great feast. As part of the preparation, the women were asked to bring the whole harvest of cactus fruit with them.

The people gathered in the valley, and at sunrise the women began cooking the cactus fruit on the fire. For the entire day the women stood over the hot fire, stirring the fruit so it wouldn't burn. Finally when the sun set, the women removed the fruit and poured it into *ollas*, big jars. The wise old men asked the people to wait four days while the cooked cactus fruit turned into wine.

When the wine was ready, the women passed it around. The four old wise men sat on the ground facing the mountains, and began to sing a very old song about the Earth. The younger men joined in the song, and danced around the wise men.

By the end of the first day, the Desert People noticed that the mountains had softened. That night while the younger men slept, the four old wise men watched the mountains and continued to sing,

The next day when the sleeping men awoke, they began to sing and dance again. The women passed the wine, and the old men urged the people to sing and dance harder than they had before.

At the end of the second day the mountains began to tremble. That night everybody stayed awake. The men continued to sing and dance. Again the women passed the wine. And so it continued through the third day. By day's end the mountains started to move.

On the fourth day, the old wise men implored the men to sing and dance with even more intensity. The men danced with renewed energy and the women passed the wine. Throughout the day the mountains slowly slid farther back.

By the time the sun went down, the mountains were moving so quickly that the peaks began to tumble and fall. Immense pieces of rock crumbled and slid down the slopes. Huge boulders flew into the air. Frightened, the men stopped singing and dancing; the women dropped the jars of wine.

The next morning when the mountains stopped their retreat and the dust settled out of the air, the people saw how far back the mountains had moved. The valley had doubled in size and there was much more good land for farming. The men, women, and children rejoiced.

Not everyone was pleased, however. The Cloud Spirit, who made his home in the mountains, saw that he now had to travel much further to get from one side of the valley to the other. He became angry and refused to carry any more water than he had before the mountains moved.

And so the beautiful valley became parched. The Desert People received their wish for more space, but now there was not enough water to turn the new land into usable fields. To this day, the desert valley blooms only when the Cloud Spirit decides to visit.

A desert is a place that receives less than 10 inches of rain a year. In summer, daytime temperatures in some deserts often soar to more than 100°F and may reach a sweltering 120°F. At night the temperature plummets because no clouds hover overhead to hold in the heat.

High mountain ranges are one cause of deserts. Along the western edge of the United States lie steep mountains that govern the wind and weather over a large part of the American West. Prevailing westerly winds force moist air from the Pacific Ocean up the slopes of these mountains. As it rises, the air quickly cools, dropping about 3.5°F for every 1,000 feet it gains in altitude.

Cool air cannot hold as much moisture as warm air. If the air cools enough, its water vapor condenses. Clouds form and rain or snow falls. Much of the moisture is wrung from the air before it passes over a mountain. As the air descends along the opposite side of the mountain, it warms. The remaining droplets evaporate. Little precipitation falls in this "rain shadow." Lush forests grow on the soggy side of mountains, but deserts form on the dry side.

As air travels eastward over the continent, it may encounter one or more additional mountain ranges. These ranges squeeze out moisture, too, but they do not receive as much as the first mountain range received.

The driest desert on Earth sits atop a layer of solid ice about 1.6 miles deep. It spans the entire continent of Antarctica. There, the frigid temperatures prevent the air from holding much moisture.

Deserts are just one kind of climate that exists on Earth. A climate describes the pattern of weather conditions for a particular region over a long period of time. Climates are classified by temperature and rainfall. Warm and moist tropical climates near the equator, and cold and dry climates near the poles are examples of other climates. Much of the United States lies in a temperate climate, which is typified by cold, wet winters and warm, moist summers.

SOURCE NOTES

[1]   The flood legend was adapted mainly from "Manabozho and the Great Serpent" by Ephraim Squier in the *American Whig Review* (October 1848), pp. 392–398, and "The Great Serpent and the Great Flood" in *Voices of the Winds: Native American Legends* by Margot Edmonds and Ella E. Clark (New York: Facts on File Publications, 1989), pp. 247–250.

[2]   The rainbow myth was based on "The Rainbow (Kee-aw-hawt)" by Harold Bell Wright in *Long Ago Told: Legends of the Papago Indians* (New York: D. Appleton, 1929), pp. 208–214.

[3]   The sun myth was adapted from "Chuhwuht: Song of the World" sung and told by Chief Visak Vo-o-yim (Hovering Hawk) in *The Indians' Book: Songs and Legends of the American Indians* by Natalie Curtis (New York: Dover Publications, 1968), pp. 315–316. Originally published by Harper and Brothers in 1923.

[4]   The wind legend comes from "Tŭmĭlkoontaoo (Broken-Wing)" by Silas Tertius Rand in *Micmac Indian Legends* (New York & London: Longmans, Green & Co., 1894), pp. 360–363.

[5]   The changing weather legend was adapted primarily from "Legends of the Slavey Indians of the Mackenzie River" by Robert Bell in the *Journal of American Folklore*, Vol. 14 (1901), pp. 26–28.

[6]   The seasons legend was adapted from "Shakok and Miochin: Origin of Summer and Winter" by George H. Pradt in the *Journal of American Folklore*, Vol. 15 (1902), pp. 88–90, and from "The North Wind and the South Wind" by Charles F. Lummis in *Pueblo Indian Folk-Stories* (Lincoln: University of Nebraska Press, 1992), originally published as *The Man Who Married the Moon, and Other Pueblo Indian Folk-Stories* (London: The Century Company, 1894).

[7]   The cloud and rain myth was adapted from "The Ants That Pushed on the Sky" by Charles Lummis, also in *Pueblo Indian Folk-Stories*, pp. 147–160.

[8]   The Indian summer myth came from "Penobscot Tales" by Frank G. Speck in the *Journal of American Folklore*, Vol. 48 (1935), pp. 95–96.

[9]   The thunder, lightning, and tornado myth was inspired by "Thunder Horse" in *Stories of the Sioux* by Herbert Morton Stoops (Boston & New York: Houghton Mifflin, 1934), pp. 75–76, and "Thunderhead Mountains" recorded by James LaPointe in *Legends of the Lakota* (San Francisco: The Indian Historian Press, 1976), pp. 59–63.

[10] The drought and climate myth is a retelling of "The Fields (Aw-oi-tuck)" found in *Long Ago Told* on pages 135–140. In his introduction to the book, Wright acknowledged the help of two members of the Papago tribe—Richard Hendricks and Muh-leef Chee-awch, also known as Hugh Norris.

I waded through vast amounts of source material in researching this book. I found the publications by Ella E. Clark to be the most useful. Clark was interested in legends of earth and sky, and she had a keen sense of story. Often I used her references as a guide to finding original source material. Ella Clark was the author of *Indian Legends of the Pacific Northwest* (Berkeley: University of California Press, 1953), *Indian Legends from the Northern Rockies* (Norman: University of Oklahoma Press, 1966), *Indian Legends of Canada* (Toronto: McClelland and Stewart, 1974), and the coauthor of *Voices of the Winds: Native American Legends* with Margot Edmonds (New York: Facts on File Publications, 1989). The last book was especially helpful.

INDEX